More Proofreading Practice, Please!

Grade 3

by Dan Greenberg

New York • Toronto • London • Auckland • Sydney
Mexico City • New Delhi • Hong Kong • Buenos Aires

Cover design by Gerard Fuchs
Cover illustration by Larry Jones
Interior design by Creative Pages, Inc.
Interior illustrations by Mike Moran

ISBN 0-439-18839-3

Printed in the U.S.A.
3 4 5 6 7 8 9 10 40 10 09

Contents

Introduction

Do you need a book that helps students master the skills of proofreading? To find out if you are ready for *More Proofreading Practice, Please!* take this handy quiz:

1. My students typically proofread their work

Ⓐ sometimes

Ⓑ only on weekends

Ⓒ when pigs have wings

Ⓓ Are you kidding?

2. Proofreading is an important part of the writing process and provides students with

Ⓐ 12 vitamins and minerals

Ⓑ a whole new outlook on the world

Ⓒ an excuse for why their writing needs help

Ⓓ Are you kidding?

3. A proofreading error was the cause of

Ⓐ the War of 1812

Ⓑ the stock market crash of 1929

Ⓒ reality TV

Ⓓ Are you kidding?

Scoring

If you answered D. *Are you kidding?* to all of the above, you're ready for *More Proofreading Practice, Please!* In fact, if you didn't answer *D* above, you're also ready for the book. In general, you need *More Proofreading Practice, Please!* if:

- your students have never heard of proofreading.
- your students have heard of proofreading, but would rather shovel out horse stables with a grapefruit spoon than take the time to proofread their work.
- your students prefer stories, poems, articles, and essays that are engaging, fun, and delightful rather than tedious, dull, and pointless.
- your students like to laugh while they're learning and learn while they're laughing.
- your students need to practice proofreading and editing skills that include punctuation, capitalization, spelling, and grammar skills.

How to Use This Book

The book is organized into four proofreading subject areas: Spelling, Punctuation and Capitalization, Grammar, and Mixed Errors. Each section includes nine activities.

The Spelling section includes topics such as plurals and homophones. Within the Punctuation and Capitalization section, topics such as proper nouns, possessives, contractions, and comma usage are covered. The Grammar section covers subject-verb agreement, tenses, sentence fragments, and more. The final section invites students to make corrections in all major categories, testing their mastery of proofreading rules.

Selections—in the form of stories, essays, poems, ads, forms, brochures, editorials, diaries, and so on—are presented in a way that allows students to make proofreading corrections right on the page using proofreading symbols. (A reproducible page of common proofreading symbols is provided on page 6.) Be sure to go over how to use these symbols. Annotated answers to each exercise are given at the end of the book.

Classroom Management

Selections in this book can be:

- distributed and completed on an individual basis.
- done as a class with you eliciting volunteer responses.
- assigned as work for partners or small cooperative groups to complete.
- distributed for homework or in-class work.
- completed as part of a Writing Program or Writing Lab.
- incorporated as part of a Five-Step Writing Process program that includes Prewriting, Drafting, Revising, Proofreading, and Publishing.

You might also try:

- having students trade writing samples and proofread each other's work.
- having students proofread papers that they have written for other subjects, such as social studies, science, or math.
- playing a proofreading game in which students are challenged to find, for example, "all 27 errors in this article."

Going Beyond

The true test of proofreading exercises is whether they carry over into students' own writing. To find out, ask students to write their own selections (based on selections in this book!) and proofread them. Stress that proofreading should include not only correcting errors, but also paying attention to the content and structure of the writing and making sure that all ideas are expressed as clearly and succinctly as possible.

Most of All

Try to make proofreading a fun part of the writing process that students look forward to doing, rather than a chore that hangs over their heads. Point out that the selections in this book become clearer, and thus more interesting, engaging, and *funny* only after they are proofread and minor errors are eliminated.

Proofreading Symbols

	Example	Symbol	Meaning
	a ~~big~~ dog	ɣ	Delete (Take it away forever!)
	~~dug~~ (dog)	^—	Delete and change to something else
¶	Once upon a time	¶	Begin a new paragraph
(lc)	I ~~L~~ove socks	(lc)	Lowercase that capital letter
(cap)	in miami, Florida	(cap)	Capitalize that lowercase letter
	Ames, Iowa	^,	Insert comma
	"What's up?" Fred asked.	" "	Insert quotation marks
	The cat sat on the mat.	⊙	Insert period
	What time is it?	?	Insert question mark
	The dog adorable wagged its tail.	∿	Transpose (or trade positions)

Name ______________________________ Date ______________

Garage Sale

Find and mark the ten spelling errors.

We have grate stuff and big bargains!

Office Supplys

- Big boxes of old newspaper
- Ballpoint pens that are out of ink
- Broken rubber bands
- Empty printer ink containers

Clothing

- Singel left shoes
- Socks with hoales
- Jackets with broken zippers
- Sleeves that were cut off a shirt

Household Goods

- Old phon books
- Torn sheets
- Old toothbrushes
- Empty pante cans
- Chipped plates
- A bunch of old pizza boxs

Ferniture and Hardware

- A big box of bent nails
- A saggy bed
- A sofa with mice living in it
- A chare with only three legs
- A TV with only one channel
- Old dor knobs

Name ________________________________ Date ______________

How to "Ride" a Poem

Find and mark the ten spelling errors.

Writeing a poem
Is like riding a bike.
Once you start riding
You ride where you like.

For exampel, I can write
Any wurd I want here
As long as it rhymes
And soundes good to the ear.

I can write in any style
I can write in any spede
As long as my readrs
Continue to read.

There'is only one danger
One risk that I run
When I sense that my readers
Have stoped having fun.

At this point its' best
Not to delay.
Simply kick up your kickstand
And just ride eway.

Name ________________________ Date ____________

The Oatmeal Council Presents: Healthy Eating With Oatmeal

Find and mark the ten spelling errors.

Here are some new recipes you'ill love that feature the healthfle benefits of oatmeal. Try them soon!

Grilled Oatmeal-Ooze Burgers

Shape oatmeal into patties. Place on a grill. Cook until it oozes out and falls on the charcoal. Skrape from charcoal and eat.

Oatmeal Cone

Scoop out frozen oatmeal onto a sugar cone. Top with colurful oatmeal sprinkles. Enjoy this trete!

Oatmeal in a Big Garbage Can

Dump a bunch of oatmeal into a garbage can. Stir, useing a garden shovel. Spune into bowls and eat.

Rock Hard Oatmeal Surprise Balls

Make hollow balls out of oatmeal. Cook until rock hard. Then fill with more oatmeal. Cook ugin until rock hard. Then coat with a layer of oatmeel on the outside. It'is delicious!

Name ______________________________ Date ______________

U.S. Census, Page 41

Find and mark the ten spelling errors.

Page 41, the final page of the U.S. Census form, is about how Americans live today. Here are some of the questions from page 41.

1. Have you, at any time during the past 12 monthes

- __ had a donkey living in your home?
- __ laughed so hard that milk came out of your noze?
- __ tryed to talk to a squirrel?

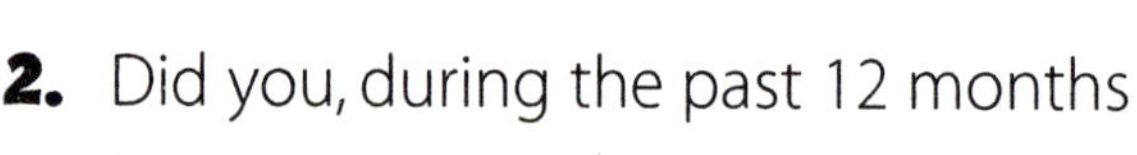

2. Did you, during the past 12 months

- __ make truck noises as you walked down the streat?
- __ eat pizza for more than seven meals in a row?
- __ comb your har with a fork?

3. During the past 12 months, have you thought about

- __ how big you're feet are?
- __ changeing your name to "Bobo"?
- __ how the letter "L" looks like a hockey stik?

4. Have you considered, in the past 12 months

- __ taking a bath or a showher?
- __ tying your shoes together while they'r still on your feet?
- __ wearing your ice skates to bed?

Name ______________________ Date ____________

How to Get to My Birthday Party

by Polly Esther

Find and mark the ten spelling errors.

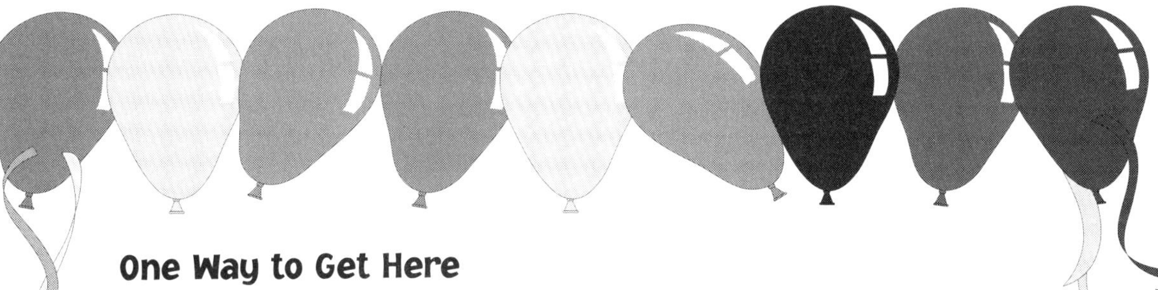

One Way to Get Here

If you're coming from the sowth, get on Webster Avenue. Make a left tern at Digger Lane. Go straight until you see a sign for Music World CDs. While yo'ure at it, check out the new CD by Elena Chuff, *Enough Is Enough*. It would make a great birthday gift! Then turn left and go down Webster until you see my house.

Another Way to Get Here

If you're coming from the east or west, turn write at North Avenue and go doun the hill until you see the sign for Bee-Bop's Comics. They have a terrific selection of comics and toys that make wonderful gifts. Keap going to Webster and follow the signs until you see my house.

Try This Way to Get Here

If you're comming from the narth, you have a great chance to stop at Teen Queen and check out the new fashions. Guess what? They're not really that expensive! Not that I really need anything like that for my birthday! Houevver, I would like a jacket. I'd also like a bracelet. Oh yeah—my house is on Webster. You can'ot miss it.

Name ______________________ Date ____________

101 New Uses for Mustard

Find and mark the ten spelling errors.

Use #8: Spread mustard on your basball glove. For some reason, the ball you use may turn a dull yellow color.

Use #14: Use mustard enstead of library paist. This is good for school projects. It doesn't really stick very well. But it's better than nothing. Then again, maybe it is'nt.

Use #27: Peannut butter and mustard sandwich. It looks awful. It tastes worse.

Use #46: Put mustard on the bottoms of your shoes. This makes a big mess. You'll track mustard all over the house. I don't know whie you'd want to do this.

Use #75: Bruch your teeth with mustard. This turns your teeth really yellow.

Use #79: Give out mustard as Halloween trets. Just hope that trick-or-treaters dont notice.

Use #100: Put mustard in your hair. You might sturt a new fad!

Name ______________________ Date ____________

Signs of the Times

Find and mark the ten spelling errors.

Sign in a school cafeteria:

Please do not use the chicken nuggetes to pownd nales,

boards, or any other hard objects.

Sign in a meeting room:

Blab-Free Zoane
Please do not blaber on so long that no one else

gets to say a werd.

Sign after Halloween:

Pumpkin-Free Zone
Pleese do not leaf pumpkins on your front

steppe after Halloween. They go soft and mak a big mess.

Name ________________________ Date ____________

Warnings That You Read in the Fine Print

Find and mark the ten spelling errors.

Warning: Photos from this camara could turn out bad if

(a) you ame the camera at your feet.

(b) you get pizza smeared on the camera lens.

(c) the purson you take a picture of is wearing a bag over his head.

You may have troubl playing with this racket if

(a) you have no tennis-playing skill.

(b) the person you're playing uhgainst does have skill.

(c) you're holding the wrong end of the racket.

This stapler may not work correctly if

(a) you try to use it underrwwater.

(b) you try to staple two rocks together.

(c) you fill it with panncak batter.

Peopil drinking this water may find

(a) that it looks just like tap water.

(b) that it tasts just like tap water.

(c) that it *is* tape water.

Name ______________________________ Date ______________

How to Solve Common Computer Problems

Find and mark the ten spelling errors.

If your computer screen freezes:

1. Yell and screme at the screen.
2. Push a lot of buttons on the computer.
3. If possible, blam the problem on someone who used the computer before you.
4. Call sombody who knows about computers.
5. Repeat steps 1–3 above.

If the screen says "Unable to Lode Program":

1. Blaime it on the program.
2. Say, "The same thing happened yesterday."
3. Push lots of buttons on your computer.
4. Call sumone who has the same problem as you.
5. Ask that person to call someone who knows about computers.
6. Repeat steps 1–3 above.

If smoke starts pouring out of your computer:

1. Yell, "Smoke is comeing out of my computer!"
2. Undplug the computer.
3. Wait 30 seconds.
4. Go to the nearestt computer store and bye a new computer.
5. If your new computer starts to smoke, repeat steps 1–4.

Name ______________________________ Date ______________

When I Grow Up, Here's What I'd Like . . .

Find and mark the ten punctuation and capitalization errors.

Sylvia P. said, "when I grow up, I'll have a hamster. His name will be Winston. Every night he'll eat dinner with me at the dinner table using a tiny fork and knife"

Ralphie G. said, I'd like to be a football player with a hurt fingernail. I'd wear cool sunglasses after the game."

Rosa R. said, "What would I like when I grow up. I'd like to speak twelve different languages and be a multi-billionaire. Or, I'd like to work in a pizza shop."

Horatio C. said, "I'd be a movie star? I'd have big muscles and a diamond earring. but I'd only wear the earring in one ear."

Jill L. said, "I'd be a Scientist who invented something really important. I'd invent a new color and I'd call it 'swack.' It would be sort of pinkish-brown."

Quinn Q. said, "I'd be a fashion designer. I'd have my own company, wear boots and have my own truck."

Elvin v. said, "I'd have a whole bathtub filled with corn chips. I might have some tortilla chips, too.

Name ______________________________ Date ______________

Crocodile Critter Sports Drink Letter

Find and mark the ten punctuation and capitalization errors.

Monica Beesley
President
Crocodile Critter Sports Drink Company
Spillway, florida 32888

dear Ms. Beesley,

You should be ashamed of yourself! your ads show gold medal-winning MVP soccer star Liz lizzley. Your ads say I'll be just like Liz if i drink Crocodile Critter Sports Drink
So I drank some, but I didn't win any gold medals. I didn't get any MVP votes, either. in fact, nothing really happened. I want my money back!

Sincerely,
Mona Meek

P.S. Crocodile Critter doesn't taste one bit like crocodiles, Either. What do you put in it!

Name ______________________________ Date ______________

Crocodile Critter Sports Drink Answer

Find and mark the ten punctuation and capitalization errors.

Monica Beesley
President
Crocodile Critter Sports Drink Company
Spillway, Florida 32888

Mona meek
66 Central Street
Sunshine, California 94441

Dear Ms. Meek,

first, I want to apologize to you from all of us at Crocodile Critter. I also want to assure you that Crocodile Critter is made from the finest fake ingredients. We do not use any Real crocodiles to make our Drink

Second, we never promised that you would be like liz lizzley if you drank Crocodile Critter. The fine print on the label says:

> Crocodile Critter is little more than sugar water with green food coloring. It will not make you a better athlete It will not make you a better person. If you think it will, you are wrong?

I hope this clears things up for you,

Sincerely,
Monica Beesley, President

Name ______________________ Date ____________

Why I Don't Like Weasels

by Louie the Dog

Find and mark the ten punctuation and capitalization errors.

Reason 1: Weasels are sneaky.

Hey, I don't sneak around. you don't sneak around. So why should weasels. They shouldn't, and that's why I don't like them.

Reason 2: Weasels smell like weasels.

No offense, but weasels smell awful. They do? That's another Reason why I don't care for them.

Reason 3: Weasels slink around like weasels?

Why don't they stand up straight? Why don't they wag their tails! What's wrong with them, anyway? Why are they always slinking around like Weasels?

Reason 4: You can't trust a weasel.

You just can't. that's all there is to it.

Reason 5: Weasels cause earthquakes.

I can't prove this, but have you ever seen a weasel during an earthquake in alaska? Of course not, because they know it's coming, and they're hiding out.

Reason 6: No one likes weasels.

Do you like weasels! I don't. Name one good thing that weasels do. I bet you can't.

Scholastic Professional Books *More Proofreading Practice, Please! Grade 3*

Name ______________________________ Date ______________

Editorial: My Turn

Find and mark the ten punctuation and capitalization errors.

Recently, i have heard the cry go up to put all my Stuffed animals away in the closet. You've heard the reasons stated by my critics. They say my stuffed animals are taking up too much space? They say I'm too old for stuffed animals. They say a lot of things.

I'd like to take this chance to answer by making a statement of my own. after careful thought, I have decided not to put my stuffed animals away in the closet. The reason is simple It's just too sad and lonely in there!

I know how my critics might respond to this claim They'll say, stuffed animals are not Real. Stuffed animals are nothing but cloth and sawdust." My response is, "so what? I still love the little critters." And even if they don't have brains, they're still my friends. You just don't put your friends in the closet.

Name ______________________________ Date ______________

The Best Excuses of the Year

Find and mark the ten punctuation and capitalization errors.

Best excuse for not practicing the piano:

Heather Bennett said, "i couldn't find the piano. I must have misplaced it somewhere in the house.

Best excuse for eating all of the homemade cookies:

Marco Zeno said, "They would have attracted ants. I had to eat them all? we would have been overrun by ants. I saved us."

Best excuse for not mowing the lawn:

andy Stern said, I injured my leg while eating a toasted cheese sandwich."

Best excuse for not cleaning your room:

Ho Kwan said, "It would be murder. Millions of tiny germs are feeding on the Peanut Butter sandwiches I left in there. I don't want to risk killing them by cleaning up."

Best excuse for not walking the dog:

Barbara Noffs Said, "My dog is afraid of dinosaurs. and there could be one out there."

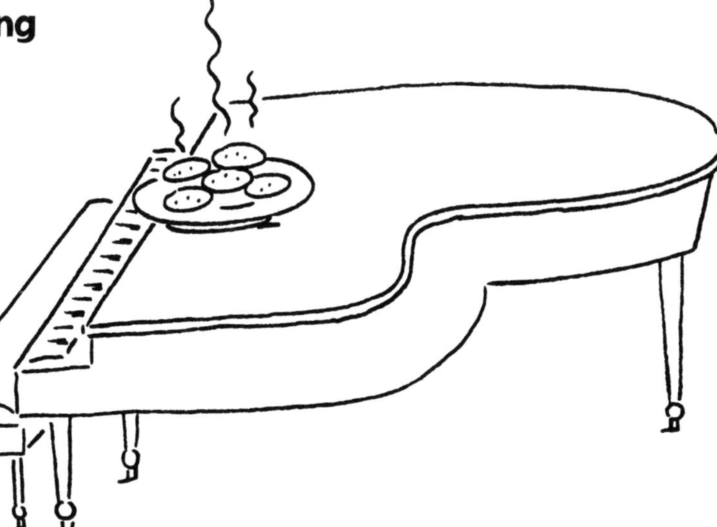

Name ______________________________ Date ______________

The Ketchup Council Presents New Ketchup Recipes

Find and mark the ten punctuation and capitalization errors.

Ketchup Mess

1. Pour 4 ounces of ketchup into four different bowls.
2. Empty the ketchup from each bowl into one big bowl?
3. Pour the ketchup from the big bowl back into the four smaller bowls.
4. repeat the process until you get really sick of it.

Ketchup Angel Food Cake

1. Whip 1 quart of ketchup for 1 hour or until your arm hurts.
2. Add 2 ounces of Dried ketchup.
3. Add 3 ounces of creamed, ketchup,
4. Cook until it starts looking like angel food cake.

Green Ketchup

1. Empty a jar of ketchup into a bowl.
2. Add Green food coloring to the ketchup.
3. Stir until it turns brown.
4. Serve with orange hamburgers, purple French fries, and blue hot dogs,

Buried Ketchup Surprise

1. Pour a bunch of ketchup into an old bucket.
2. Dig a big hole in the backyard.
3. bury the bucket.
4. Come back in september or april. Dig up the ketchup. Serve it with year-old meat loaf. It is delicious!

Name ______________________________ Date ______________

The Hairies: Hair Awards for Hollywood Movies

Find and mark the ten punctuation and capitalization errors.

Here are the winners of this year's awards for hair in american movies.

Best New Hair in a Comedy

This award goes to Steve Drooper, who played Uncle farkus in the movie "Get Me Out of Hair!" Steve's co-star, Val Vinks, says, "I like Steve's Hair."

Most Shiny Hair in a Drama

Maria Cruz wins this award for the second time? Maria says, "This is the best thing that has ever happened to my hair.

Biggest Hair in a Comedy

This award goes to Cindy Piffle. Her hair was over 3 feet tall in the movie "Eat These Beans." We couldn't see the award because Cindy's hair was in the way

Best Supporting Hair

Sometimes hair is not the star of the movie. it plays a supporting, or helping, role. Val vinks wins for "Get Me Out of Hair!"

Best Overall Hair

This is the big one! The award for the best hair for the entire year went to steve Drooper. Double winner Steve sobbed, I can't believe it. I never could have played this part without my hair."

Scholastic Professional Books *More Proofreading Practice, Please!* Grade 3

Name ______________________________ Date ______________

Clock Creations: New Ideas for Clocks

Find and mark the ten punctuation and capitalization errors.

The Smell Clock

Each hour has a different smell. It smells like Bacon and Eggs at 7:00 A.M. It smells like old gym socks at 4:00 P.M. to tell you it's time to exercise. At 8:30 P.M., the smell of shampoo tells you it is time to bathe?

The Wrong Time Clock

Do you not like to know what time it is. This clock won't cramp your style. it always shows the wrong time, night and day.

The Nag Clock

Push the button. It nags. For example, it might say, "hurry up! You're late! You're going to miss the Bus!"

The Slow/Fast Clock

this clock runs fast when you're doing something boring. Then it slows down when you're having fun!

Backwards Clock

It runs backwards. Twelve o'clock is followed by eleven. This is for people who don't care about how much time has passed. They want to know how much time is left

Stop Clock

Do you have a favorite time of day. This clock stays stuck on your favorite time. It's easy to set, and it never needs batteries!

Name ______________________________ Date ______________

Ratings

Find and mark the ten grammar errors.

- **This film has been rated DUH-9.**

Viewer nine and under will find this movie dull and silly. Viewers *over* the age of nine will also find this movie dull and silly. The film is recommended for all other viewers'.

- **This weekend has been rated NHW-18.**

There is no homework for all student under eighteen. This homework ban will last for the whole weekend. Anyone caught doing homework must stop and play two video game.

- **This cereal has been rated TMMF-Minus.**

It have too many marshmallows and not enough taste. To make it healthy, add milk to cereal. You should remove the cereal from the bowl. Drinking the milk.

- **This book has been rated WC.**

It's way cool. It's exciting and funny. You'll love it. What is you waiting for?

- **This music video has been rated FA-100.**

It is totally, 100 percent fake. The singing was dubbed. The dancing was done by hired actor's. The music was canned. Even the crowd was paid to cheer.

- **This puppy has been rated AD-100.**

She is 100 percent adorable. She is cute or playful. You will love her. We are not responsible for any mess this one puppies might make.

Name ________________________ Date ____________

Movie Capsules

Find and mark the ten grammar errors.

Titanic 3

The movie asks the questions, "What would have happened if all of the crew and the passengers aboard the *H.M.S. Titanic* were chimpanzees?" It were a promising idea, but in the end it just sinks.

Timmy for President

Six-year-old Timmy Whipple gets elected presidents. Everything are great until Timmy cries at the toy store.

Unlikely Romance

She is an actor. He are an evil man. Them meet and fall in love. She learn that he is really a painter. Then he have her arrested. By the end, you'll be so confused you won't care what happens.

Fungus

What if mushrooms could talk? What would they say? This movie answers the question. Mushroom's wouldn't say much at all. They had probably just sit there.

Name ______________________________ Date ______________

The Rules of Cool

by Thelonious LeGroove

Find and mark the ten grammar errors.

Folks say to me all the time, "How done you stay so cool?" I tell them, "That is none of your business!" But them don't like that. So I've come up with the Rules of Cool.

Rule 1 You should wear sunglasses. Because shades are cool. Wear them everywhere, including in the bathtub.

Rule 2 You should look bored. Being bored am cool. Yawning shows that you are cool.

Rule 3 You shouldn't say much. Just sit there, wear your shade's, and be cool.

Rule 4 You should use cool words. "Like" and "ville" are cool words. Here are a good example. "I'm, like, really hungry. Let's, like, go to lunch-ville."

Rule 5 You shouldn't wear superhero underwear. You may think it be cool, but it isn't. Trust me on this one.

Rule 6 If you need to read these rules, then you is probably not cool. You never will be. Cool people don't follow rules. They make the rule's!

Name ______________________ Date ______________

Highlights of the Speeches at the Hamster Convention

Find and mark the ten grammar errors.

Martha Washington Hamster

"Fellow hamsters, the time has come for freedom! We would not live in cages! We will not eat little food pellets! Us will not drink out of water bottles! Give us liberty, or give us nothing!"

Alexander Hamster

"Hear this, people of the world, hamsters is tired! We are tired of being pet. We are tired of being held. We are tired of being call cute. We are no longer your pets! We want jobs! We want rights!"

Dollie Hamster

"My fellow hamsters, the enemy is near. We know who they really is. Them are cats! They say they just want to sleep and eat my cat food. But I have seen the look in their eyes. Watch out for all purring sounds!"

Woodrow Wilson Hamster

"We have a good thing here! We get free food! We get plastic houses! We get petted! Is you willing to throw all this away? What will you do with this freedom? Will you walk through a house full of cats? Where will you find food? Where will you hide? Be glad you is a pet!"

Name ______________________________ Date ______________

Predictions That Never Came True

Find and mark the ten grammar errors.

The following predictions were made by Magda the Magic, the Great Steve, and Rowena the Wise. None of them came true.

☐ **True**
☑ **Not True**

The Great Steve said, "Early next year, a hairbrush will be elected President of the United States."

☐ **True**
☑ **Not True**

Magda the Magic say, "A new law will be past that gets rid of all Tuesdays and Thursdays. The new days of the week will be Sunday, Monday, Monday Again, Wednesday, Another Wednesday, Friday, and Saturday."

☐ **True**
☑ **Not True**

Rowena the Wise said, "A team of 10-year-old childs will win the Super Bowl. They will. Beat the Green Bay Packers in a close game."

☐ **True**
☑ **Not True**

Magda the Magic said, "Scientists will learn that chickens is smarter than human beings. A chicken will run for president and lose in a close races."

☐ **True**
☑ **Not True**

The Great Steve said, "The new fad for children will be cheese dolls. These dolls will have chubby bodies and these dolls will be made of cheese, and these dolls will make good snacks."

Scholastic Professional Books *More Proofreading Practice, Please!* Grade 3

Name ______________________________ Date ________________

Doorknob Q & A

Find and mark the ten grammar errors.

Many people today is confused about doorknobs. This page gives the facts about doorknobs.

Question: Why are doorknobs important?

Answer: Doorknobs are important because it open doors. If you don't believe this, try opening a door without a doorknob. You'll see how important doorknobs be.

Question: My friend Mary is getting a doorknob for his birthday. Should I got one too?

Answer: Getting your first doorknob is important. Discuss the matter with your parents, a close friend, or a stranger passing by on the street.

Question: Why isn't more doorknobs shaped like bananas or other fruits?

Answer: People might mistake them for real fruits and try to eat they. This could be dangerous.

Question: Does doorknobs really grow on trees?

Answer: There are doorknob bushes that grow in South America. Most of the doorknobs that grow there are small and didn't fit on doors in the United States.

Question: If doorknobs could talk, what would they say?

Answer: One would probably say, "Please turn me. I'm a doorknobs." Then again, it might say something completely different.

Scholastic Professional Books *More Proofreading Practice, Please! Grade 3*

Name ______________________ Date ______________

Your Horoscope

Find and mark the ten grammar errors.

Aquarius: Your sun am lined up with your moon. That means your ballpoint pen will run out of ink. You will also fall in love—with a turtles!

Pisces: Do you remember that one things that you really wanted? Today will be the day that you get it. Then again, it might not. It all depends.

Scorpio: You leaved the back door open. Go close it. Hurry!

Taurus: It be a bad day for a pony ride. If you feel like riding a pony, don't do it. Try riding a bicycle instead, or maybe a largest dogs.

Sagittarius: Don't even think of leaving any hundred-dollar bills lying around the house. You could lose it.

Libra: Your plans for baking a 150-layer cake may have to be delayed. You should think smaller.

The Rest of the Signs: Today are your lucky day. Don't be surprised if someone walking up and hands you one million dollars. Stay away from false horoscopes. They are not true.

Name ______________________ Date ____________

Dr. Lorna, Pet Psychologist

Find and mark the ten grammar errors.

Dear Dr. Lorna,

Me need your help. My turtle, Willie, are shy. I can't get him to come out of her shell. What should I do?

Signed,
Turtle Lover

Dear Shy,

Turtles are stubborn creature. They rarely come out of them shells. Look for events that might interest a turtle, such as basking in the sun or an egg-laying party.

Dr. Lorna

Dear Dr. Lorna,

My teenage cat Sniffles sleeped all day. She won't helped around the house. She won't even watch TV. All she does is sleep and go out to see their friends at night. Should I be worried?

Signed,
Worried in Wooster

Dear Worried,

Teenage cats is known for being lazy. Try putting a sprig of catnip under your cats nose. You will be amazed!

Dr. Lorna

Name ______________________________ Date ______________

New Museums Around Town

Find and mark the ten grammar errors.

The Museum of Gum

Did you know that there is over 1,500 different kinds of gum? You can seen them all in this museum. It includes NBC (Never Been Chewed) gum, ABC (Already Been Chewed) gum displays. Try the cafeteria. There is a complete menu of gum choices for lunch.

The Macaroni Art Museum

This great museum has masterpieces of macaroni art. Some are sprayed with gold. silver paint. There is other kinds of pasta, including spaghetti, little shells, and of course, wagon wheels.

One Billion Dollars

This is not really a museum. It's just a billion dollars in a bigger bag. If you pay extra you can roll around in the money.

The Broken TV and Radio Museum

There are thousands of broken television and radio here. We are proud that none of them work.

Art That Is So Bad You Could Have Made It Yourself

A museum that have lots of important art. The art is so bad that you could have made it itself. You can see finger painting, blobs, smears, and others.

Name ______________________________ Date ______________

Little Red Riding Hood

Find and mark the twelve errors. They may be spelling, punctuation, capitalization, or grammar errors.

Little Red Riding Hood lived in the forest. One day her mother tell her to take a pot of tee and three tiny cakes to her granny.

Along came a wolf.

"Who are you." Red asked.

"I'm a wolf," said the wolf.

"A wolf?" said Red. "What's a wolf?"

"Never mind," said the wolf. "If you don't wach out, I'll blow your house down!

At that point, three pigs came running out of their houses. "Is this guy bothering you?" they ask.

"I'm not sure," said Red. "He told me he was going to bloe my house down."

"he could'nt even blow his own nose," said the pigs.

"Oh yeah?" said the wolf. "Watch this."

Well, he blew the house down. But it wasn't Red's house. it was Granny's house and Granny was hopping mad.

"Who did this?" Granny cried.

Red and the three pig pointed at the wolf.

"I'm sorry," said the wolf. "I was just trying to prove a point."

"Here, Granny," said Red, handing her the tea and cakes. "They'll make you feel better."

So, the wolf and Granny had tea and cakes.

Name ______________________________ Date ________________

Diary of a Dog

by Louie the Dog

Find and mark the twelve errors. They may be spelling, punctuation, capitalization, or grammar errors.

Dear Diary,

Today I get up. I did some scrathing because my neck itched. Then I slept. Then I did some sniffing around. Then I slept. Then I barked at the maillman. After that, I took a nap until dinnertime. for dinner, I had pellets in a dish. then I went back to sleep.

Yours truly, **Louie**

Dear Diary,

Today I saw a small white cats out in the yard. This really made me mad! So I barked a lot. I felt better afterwards. Do you know what I ate for dinner. I ate pellets! I washed it all down with a big slirp of water. Then I go back to sleep.

Yours truly, **Louie**

Dear Diary,

I just felt like barking todae. So I barked and barked. Then I eaten pellets and went to sleep.

Yours truly, **Louie**

Dear Diary,

That mailman comes every day! I'm getting tired of barking at him. But I did it anyway? Also, I took a walk. Tomorrow I'll catch up on my sleeping.

Yours truly, **Louie**

Name ______________________________ Date ______________

Masterpiece Art

Find and mark the twelve errors. They may be spelling, punctuation, capitalization, or grammar errors.

An Interview with Winnie Van Wonk

Winnie Van Wonk is truly won of the great masters. You look at her work and you are amazed. It wiggils its ears. It seems to be alive! How does she do it?

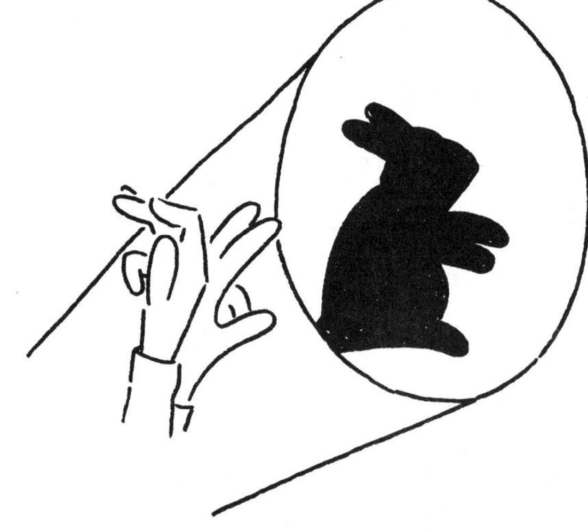

I visited Van Wonk's exhibit in Toledo, ohio, on friday. I asked she, "How do you do it."

"It's all in the way you hold your hands," she said. She show me the secret. I couldn't believe it!

Then I asked, "Wha'is next?" She showwed me her's new creation.

"I call it the swan," Van Wonk said to I.

What a genius!" I thought. I still feel that way today!

Name ________________________ Date ____________

The Oatmeal Council Presents: New Oatmeal Products

Find and mark the twelve errors. They may be spelling, punctuation, capitalization, or grammar errors.

Here is some great knew oatmeal products. try them soon!

Oatmeal Sneakers

These are high quality athletic shoes maid of oatmeal. You should not exercise on a field that contains milk and butter Your shoes could turn to mush.

Oatmeal Computer

Imagine an entire computers made of oatmeal. The monitor: hard drive, and modem are all oatmeal. Because it is made of oatmeal, this computer do not work at all.

Oatmeal Tennis Balls

Play Tennis with balls made of oatmeal. After a few swats, watch the oatmeal fly! It will make you want to play a game at breakfast thyme.

Oatmeal Snow Tires

Mount the tires on your car and go! This great for both trucks and cars! What's the best thing about this? If you get hungy, you can just eat your tires!

Scholastic Professional Books *More Proofreading Practice, Please! Grade 3*

Name ______________________________ Date ________________

More Predictions That Never Came True

Find and mark the twelve errors. They may be spelling, punctuation, capitalization, or grammar errors.

The following predictions were made by Magda the Magic, the Great Steve, and Rowena the Wise last year. None of them came true.

☐ True
☑ Not True

Rowena the Wise said, "restaurants will surve pills instead of food. You'ill be able to get a full meal made completele of pills. It will be delicious."

☐ True
☑ Not True

Magda the Magic say, "A band of squirrels will go on a bank-robbing spree and steal millions of dollars. The money will be found in a hollow tree. The squirrels won't never be caught."

☐ True
☑ Not True

The Great steve said, The sun will not rise in the east one morning. It will rise in the north. It will be two hours late. After that, they will learn its lesson and be on time from then on."

☐ True
☑ Not True

Magda the Magic said, "Scientists will discover that fire is actually cold. Campfires will replace air conditioners to keep houses cool"

☐ True
☑ Not True

Rowena the Wise said, "The words 'hello' and 'good-bye' will switch places. 'Hello' will be used to say good-bye to people. And 'good-bye' will be used to say 'hello.' Hello, I must go now."

Scholastic Professional Books *More Proofreading Practice, Please!* Grade 3

Name ______________________________ Date ______________

Playground Sports Report

Find and mark the twelve errors. They may be spelling, punctuation, capitalization, or grammar errors.

Welcome to the Oakland Plaground Sports Report, where we keep you posted on playground sports events.

In hopscotch, Lance Yee hopped and hopped. Then he fall down. "It's not fair!" said Yee.

In dodge ball, Cindy Brill got hit on the leg by a ball throne by Tommy Finster. "You're out!" cried Finster. "it didn't hurt a bit," Brill said afterward.

In kickball, Joey Wankel got mad when he didn't get picked for the green team. So he took its ball and went home.

During the morning kickball game, Ginny Pfaff call Timmy Quigley a bad name. Quigley said, "Sticks and stones may brake my bones, but names will never hurt me"

On the jungle gym, Sabrina Sykes did climbed what is now being described as "really, really high." Said Sykes, "That was really, really high!"

On the swigs, Billy Carbury went back and forth a bunch of times. Carbury said, That was really fun".

Name ____________________________ Date ______________

This Day in History

Find and mark the twelve errors. They may be spelling, punctuation, capitalization, or grammar errors.

One Year Ago

National Eat Lunch with a Tree Day was declared a holiday on monday, April 2. No one has figureed out how you would actually eat lunch with a tree. If they do, this will be a great celebration.

37 Years Ago

The excuse, "The dog ate my homwork" was first used by Timmy Murtz of ogden, ohio. Timmy don't actually have a dog—or any homework, for that matter! His techer didn't believe the excuse for even one second.

50 Years Ago

On august 7, the annoying telephone call were invented in Newark, New Jersey. Homeowners were called and ask if they would like a free offer.

100 Years Ago

Scientest Alexander Graham Baloney said that water is actually not wet. It just seems wet because the other things around it are very dry. His idea were later proved to be purely preposterous.

Name ______________________________ Date ________________

Things That Tape Might Fix.com

Find and mark the twelve errors. They may be spelling, punctuation, capitalization, or grammar errors.

Welcome to "Things That Tape Might Fix.com."

This is your one-stop source for finding out if tape will fix something. click on any of the choices below to discover things that tape mite fix.

Choice 1: You have capture a wild hippopotamus in the back of your truck. You plan to drive it to a safe place and set it free. But the hippo has brokken through the gate of the truck. Can you use tape to repair the gate?

Answer: Yes, but make sure that you use hippopotamus-strength tape or something stronger.

Choice 2: The dog accidentally teared up your homework. Can you use tape to put it back together again.

Answer: You can try, but it still won't change those wrong answers you wrote.

Choice 3: Humpty Dumpty sat on a wall. Humpty Dumpty have a great fall. Can tape put humpty together again?

Answer: All the king's horses and all the king's men couldnt put Humpty together again—even *with* tape.

Choice 4: Slideing into second base, you rip the knee of her jeans. Can you use tape to repair the rip

Answer: Yes, but you're still out!

Name ______________________ Date ____________

More Signs of the Times

Find and mark the twelve errors. They may be spelling, punctuation, capitalization, or grammar errors.

this sign was hung on a wall.

Please do not made shadow bunnys, birds, monkeys, people, or any other shadow figures on this wall

This sign was hung in a bedroom.

This sign were posted on a bath-room mirror.

Garage Sale, page 7

We have ~~grate~~ [great] stuff and big bargains!

Office ~~Supplys~~ [Supplies]
- Big boxes of old newspaper
- Ballpoint pens that are out of ink
- Broken rubber bands
- Empty printer ink containers

Household Goods
- Old phon[e] books
- Torn sheets
- Old toothbrushes
- Empty ~~pante~~ [paint] cans
- Chipped plates
- A bunch of old pizza box[e]s

Clothing
- Singel left shoes
- Socks with hoales
- Jackets with broken zippers
- Sleeves that were cut off a shirt

F[u]rniture and Hardware
- A box of bent nails
- A saggy bed
- A sofa with mice living in it
- A ~~chare~~ [chair] with only three legs
- A TV with only one channel
- Old do[o]r knobs

How to "Ride" a Poem, page 8

Writeing a poem
Is like riding a bike.
Once you start riding
You ride where you like.

For exampel, I can write
Any w[o]rd I want here
As long as it rhymes
And soundes good to the ear.

I can write in any style
I can write in any speel,
As long as my read[e]rs
Continue to read.
~~There's~~ [There's] only one danger
One risk that I run
When I sense that my readers
Have sto[p]ped having fun.
At this point ~~its'~~ [it's] best
Not to delay.
Simply kick up your kickstand
And just ride [a]way.

The Oatmeal Council Presents: Healthy Eating With Oatmeal, page 9

Here are some new recipes ~~you'ill~~ [you'll] love that feature the ~~healthfle~~ [healthful] benefits of oatmeal. Try them soon!

Grilled Oatmeal-Ooze Burgers
Shape oatmeal into patties. Place on a grill. Cook until it oozes out and falls on the charcoal. S[c]rape from charcoal and eat.

Oatmeal Cone
Scoop out frozen oatmeal onto a sugar cone. Top with col[o]rful oatmeal sprinkles. Enjoy this ~~trete~~ [treat]!

Oatmeal in a Big Garbage Can
Dump a bunch of oatmeal into a garbage can. Stir, useing a garden shovel. ~~Spune~~ [Spoon] into bowls and eat.

Rock Hard Oatmeal Surprise Balls
Make hollow balls out of oatmeal. Cook until rock hard. Then fill with more oatmeal. Cook ~~ugin~~ [again] until rock hard. Then coat with a layer of oatme[a]l on the outside. ~~It-is~~ [It's] delicious!

U.S. Census, Page 41, page 10

Page 41, the final page of the U.S. Census form, is about how Americans live today. Here are some of the questions from page 41.

1. Have you, at any time during the past 12 monthes
   — had a donkey living in your home?
   — laughed so hard that milk came out of your no[s]e?
   — tr[i]ed to talk to a squirrel?
2. Did you, during the past 12 months
   — make truck noises as you walked down the stre[e]t?
   — eat pizza for more than seven meals in a row?
   — comb your ha[i]r with a fork?
3. During the past 12 months, have you thought about
   — how big ~~you're~~ [your] feet are?
   — changeing your name to "Bobo"?
   — how the letter "L" looks like a hockey sti[c]k?
4. Have you considered, in the past 12 months
   — taking a bath or a showher?
   — tying your shoes together while ~~they'r~~ [they're] still on your feet?
   — wearing your ice skates to bed?

How to Get to My Birthday Party, page 11

One Way to Get Here
If you're coming from the so[u]th, get on Webster Avenue. Make a left t[u]rn at Digger Lane. Go straight until you see a sign for Music World CDs. While ~~yo'ure~~ [you're] at it, check out the new CD by Elena Chuff, Enough Is Enough. It would make a great birthday gift! Then turn left and go down Webster until you see my house.

Another Way to Get Here
If you're coming from the east or west, turn ~~write~~ [right] at North Avenue and go do[w]n the hill until you see the sign for Bee-Bop's Comics. They have a terrific selection of comics and toys that make wonderful gifts. Ke[e]p going to Webster and follow the signs until you see my house.

Try This Way to Get Here
If you're comming from the n[o]rth, you have a great chance to stop at Teen Queen and check out the new fashions. Guess what? They're not really that expensive! Not that I really need anything like that for my birthday! ~~Houevver,~~ [However,] I would like a jacket. I'd also like a bracelet. Oh yeah—my house is on Webster. You ~~can'ot~~ [can't] miss it.

101 New Uses for Mustard, page 12

Use #8: Spread mustard on your bas[e]ball glove. For some reason, the ball you use may turn a dull yellow color.

Use #14: Use mustard ~~enstead~~ [instead] of library ~~paist~~ [paste]. This is good for school projects. It doesn't really stick very well. But it's better than nothing. Then again, maybe it ~~is'nt~~ [isn't].

Use #27: Peanut butter and mustard sandwich. It looks awful. It tastes worse.

Use #46: Put mustard on the bottoms of your shoes. This makes a big mess. You'll track mustard all over the house. I don't know ~~whie~~ [why] you'd want to do this.

Use #75: Bru[s]h your teeth with mustard. This turns your teeth really yellow.

Use #79: Give out mustard as Halloween tre[a]ts. Just hope that trick-or-treaters don['t] notice.

Use #100: Put mustard in your hair. You might st[a]rt a new fad!

Signs of the Times, page 13

Sign in a school cafeteria:
Please do not use the chicken nuggets to pound ~~nales,~~ nails boards, or any other hard objects.

Sign in a meeting room:
Blab-Free Zone
Please do not blaber [b] on so long that no one else gets to say a wurd [o].

Sign after Halloween:
Pumpkin-Free Zone
Plese [a] do not ~~leaf~~ leave pumpkins on your front ~~steppe~~ step after Halloween. They go soft and mak [e] a big mess.

Warnings That You Read in the Fine Print, page 14

Warning: Photos from this camra [e] could turn out bad if
(a) you ~~ame~~ aim the camera at your feet.
(b) you get pizza smeared on the camera lens.
(c) the prson [e] you take a picture of is wearing a bag over his head.

Warning: You may have troubl [e] playing with this racket if
(a) you have no tennis-playing skill.
(b) the person you're playing ~~uhgainst~~ against does have skill.
(c) you're holding the wrong end of the racket.

Warning: This stapler may not work correctly if
(a) you try to use it ~~underrwwater~~ underwater.
(b) you try to staple two rocks together.
(c) you fill it with ~~panncak~~ pancake batter.

Warning: ~~Peopil~~ People drinking this water may find
(a) that it looks just like tap water.
(b) that it tasts [e] just like tap water.
(c) that it is taped water.

How to Solve Common Computer Problems, page 15

If your computer screen freezes:
1. Yell and ~~screme~~ scream at the screen.
2. Push a lot of buttons on the computer.
3. If possible, blam [e] the problem on someone who used the computer before you.
4. Call sombody [e] who knows about computers.
5. Repeat steps 1–3 above.

If the screen says "Unable to ~~Lode~~ Load Program":
1. Blame it on the program.
2. Say, "The same thing happened yesterday."
3. Push lots of buttons on your computer.
4. Call ~~sumone~~ someone who has the same problem as you.
5. Ask that person to call someone who knows about computers.
6. Repeat steps 1–3 above.

If smoke starts pouring out of your computer:
1. Yell, "Smoke is comeing out of my computer!"
2. Undplug the computer.
3. Wait 30 seconds.
4. Go to the nearest computer store and ~~bye~~ buy a new computer.
5. If your new computer starts to smoke, repeat steps 1–4.

When I Grow Up, Here's What I'd Like..., page 16

(cap) Sylvia P. said, "when I grow up, I'll have a hamster. His name will be Winston. Every night he'll eat dinner with me at the dinner table using a tiny fork and knife."

Ralphie G. said, I'd like to be a football player with a hurt fingernail. I'd wear cool sunglasses after the game."

Rosa R. said, "What would I like when I grow up? I'd like to speak twelve different languages and be a multi-billionaire. Or, I'd like to work in a pizza shop."

Horatio C. said, "I'd be a movie star I'd have big muscles and a diamond earring but I'd only wear the earring in one ear."

(lc) Jill L. said, "I'd be a Scientist who invented something really important. I'd invent a new color and I'd call it 'swack.' It would be sort of pinkish-brown."

Quinn Q. said, "I'd be a fashion designer. I'd have my own company, wear boots and have my own truck."

(cap) Elvin v. said, "I'd have a whole bathtub filled with corn chips. I might have some tortilla chips, too.

Crocodile Critter Sports Drink Letter, page 17

Monica Beesley
President
Crocodile Critter Sports Drink Company
(cap) Spillway, florida 32888

(cap) dear Ms. Beesley,

(cap) You should be ashamed of yourself! your ads show gold medal-winning MVP soccer star Liz lizzley. Your ads
(cap) say I'll be just like Liz if i drink Crocodile Critter Sports Drink

¶ So I drank some, but I didn't win any gold medals. I
(cap) didn't get any MVP votes, either. in fact, nothing really happened. I want my money back!

Sincerely,
Mona Meek

P.S. Crocodile Critter doesn't taste one bit like crocodiles,
(lc) Either. What do you put in it

Crocodile Critter Sports Drink Answer, page 18

(cap) Mona meek
66 Central Street
Sunshine, California 94441

Dear Ms. Meek,

(cap) first, I want to apologize to you from all of us at Crocodile Critter. I also want to assure you that Crocodile Critter is made from the finest fake ingredients. We do not
(lc) use any Real crocodiles to make our Drink (lc)

Second, we never promised that you would be like liz (cap)
(cap) lizzley if you drank Crocodile Critter. The fine print on the label says:

Crocodile Critter is little more than sugar water with green food coloring. It will not make you a better athlete It will not make you a better person.

If you think it will, you are wrong

I hope this clears things up for you

Sincerely,

Monica Beesley, President

Why I Don't Like Weasels, page 19

Reason 1: Weasels are sneaky.
Hey, I don't sneak around. you don't sneak around. So why should weasels They shouldn't, and that's why I don't like them.
Reason 2: Weasels smell like weasels.
No offense, but weasels smell awful. They do That's another Reason why I don't care for them.
Reason 3: Weasels slink around like weasels
Why don't they stand up straight? Why don't they wag their tails What's wrong with them, anyway? Why are they always slinking around like Weasels?
Reason 4: You can't trust a weasel.
You just can't. that's all there is to it.
Reason 5: Weasels cause earthquakes.
I can't prove this, but have you ever seen a weasel during an earthquake in alaska? Of course not, because they know it's coming,and they're hiding out.
Reason 6: No one likes weasels.
Do you like weasels I don't. Name one good thing that weasels do. I bet you can't.

Editorial: My Turn, page 20

Recently, i have heard the cry go up to put all my Stuffed animals away in the closet. You've heard the reasons stated by my critics. They say my stuffed animals are taking up too much space They say I'm too old for stuffed animals. They say a lot of things.

I'd like to take this chance to answer by making a statement of my own. after careful thought, I have decided not to put my stuffed animals away in the closet. The reason is simple It's just too sad and lonely in there!

I know how my critics might respond to this claim They'll say stuffed animals are not Real. Stuffed animals are nothing but cloth and sawdust." My response is, "so what? I still love the little critters." And even if they don't have brains, they're still my friends. You just don't put your friends in the closet.

The Best Excuses of the Year, page 21

Best excuse for not practicing the piano:
Heather Bennett said, "i couldn't find the piano. I must have misplaced it somewhere in the house
Best excuse for eating all of the homemade cookies:
Marco Zeno said, "They would have attracted ants. I had to eat them all we would have been overrun by ants. I saved us."
Best excuse for not mowing the lawn:
andy Stern said, I injured my leg while eating a toasted cheese sandwich."
Best excuse for not cleaning your room:
Ho Kwan said, "It would be murder. Millions of tiny germs are feeding on the Peanut Butter sandwiches I left in there. I don't want to risk killing them by cleaning up."
Best excuse for not walking the dog:
Barbara Noffs Said, "My dog is afraid of dinosaurs and there could be one out there."

The Ketchup Council Presents New Ketchup Recipes, page 22

Ketchup Mess
1. Pour 4 ounces of ketchup into four different bowls.
2. Empty the ketchup from each bowl into one big bowl
3. Pour the ketchup from the big bowl back into the four smaller bowls.
4. repeat the process until you get really sick of it.

Ketchup Angel Food Cake
1. Whip 1 quart of ketchup for 1 hour or until your arm hurts.
2. Add 2 ounces of Dried ketchup.
3. Add 3 ounces of creamed ketchup
4. Cook until it starts looking like angel food cake.

Green Ketchup
1. Empty a jar of ketchup into a bowl.
2. Add Green food coloring to the ketchup.
3. Stir until it turns brown.
4. Serve with orange hamburgers, purple French fries, and blue hot dogs

Buried Ketchup Surprise
1. Pour a bunch of ketchup into an old bucket.
2. Dig a big hole in the backyard.
3. bury the bucket.
4. Come back in september or april. Dig up the ketchup. Serve it with year-old meat loaf. It is delicious!

The Hairies: Hair Awards for Hollywood Movies, page 23

Here are the winners of this year's awards for hair in american movies.
Best New Hair in a Comedy
This award goes to Steve Drooper, who played Uncle farkus in the movie "Get Me Out of Hair!" Steve's co-star, Val Vinks, says, "I like Steve's Hair."
Most Shiny Hair in a Drama
Maria Cruz wins this award for the second time Maria says, "This is the best thing that has ever happened to my hair
Biggest Hair in a Comedy
This award goes to Cindy Piffle. Her hair was over 3 feet tall in the movie "Eat These Beans." We couldn't see the award because Cindy's hair was in the way
Best Supporting Hair
Sometimes hair is not the star of the movie. it plays a supporting, or helping, role. Val vinks wins for "Get Me Out of Hair!"
Best Overall Hair
This is the big one! The award for the best hair for the entire year went to steve Drooper. Double winner Steve sobbed, I can't believe it. I never could have played this part without my hair."

Clock Creations: New Ideas for Clocks, page 24

The Smell Clock
Each hour has a different smell. It smells like Bacon and Eggs at 7:00 A.M. It smells like old gym socks at 4:00 P.M. to tell you it's time to exercise. At 8:30 P.M., the smell of shampoo tells you it is time to bathe
The Wrong Time Clock
Do you not like to know what time it is This clock won't cramp your style. it always shows the wrong time, night and day.
The Nag Clock
Push the button. It nags. For example, it might say, "hurry up! You're late! You're going to miss the Bus!"
The Slow/Fast Clock
this clock runs fast when you're doing something boring. Then it slows down when you're having fun!
Backwards Clock
It runs backwards. Twelve o'clock is followed by eleven. This is for people who don't care about how much time has passed. They want to know how much time is left
Stop Clock
Do you have a favorite time of day This clock stays stuck on your favorite time. It's easy to set, and it never needs batteries!

Answer Key

Ratings, page 25

• This film has been rated DUH-9.
Viewer[s] nine and under will find this movie dull and silly. Viewers over the age of nine will also find this movie dull and silly. The film is recommended for all other ~~viewers~~ viewers'.

• This weekend has been rated NHW-18.
There is no homework for all student[s] under eighteen. This homework ban will last for the whole weekend. Anyone caught doing homework must stop and play two video game[s].

• This cereal has been rated TMMF-Minus.
It ~~have~~ has too many marshmallows and not enough taste. To make it healthy, add milk to cereal. You should remove the cereal from the bowl. ~~Drinking~~ Drink the milk.

• This book has been rated WC.
It's way cool. It's exciting and funny. You'll love it. What ~~is~~ are you waiting for?

• This music video has been rated FA-100.
It is totally, 100 percent fake. The singing was dubbed. The dancing was done by hired ~~actor's~~ actors. The music was canned. Even the crowd was paid to cheer.

• This puppy has been rated AD-100.
She is 100 percent adorable. She is cute ~~or~~ and playful. You will love her. We are not responsible for any mess this one ~~puppies~~ puppy might make.

Movie Capsules, page 26

Titanic 3

The movie asks the question~~,~~, "What would have happened if all of the crew and the passengers aboard the H.M.S. Titanic were chimpanzees?" It ~~were~~ was a promising idea, but in the end it just sinks.

Timmy for President

Six-year-old Timmy Whipple gets elected president~~.~~. Everything ~~are~~ is great until Timmy cries at the toy store.

Unlikely Romance

She is an actor. He ~~are~~ is an evil man. The~~m~~[y] meet and fall in love. She learn[s] that he is really a painter. Then he ~~have~~ has her arrested. By the end, you'll be so confused you won't care what happens.

Fungus

What if mushrooms could talk? What would they say? This movie answers the question. ~~Mushroom's~~ Mushrooms wouldn't say much at all. They ~~had~~ would probably just sit there.

The Rules of Cool, page 27

Folks say to me all the time, "How ~~done~~ do you stay so cool?" I tell them, "That is none of your business!" But the~~m~~[y] don't like that. So I've come up with the Rules of Cool.

Rule 1 You should wear sunglasses~~/B~~ because shades are cool. Wear them everywhere, including in the bathtub. (lc)

Rule 2 You should look bored. Being bored ~~am~~ is cool. Yawning shows that you are cool.

Rule 3 You shouldn't say much. Just sit there, wear your ~~shade's~~ shades, and be cool.

Rule 4 You should use cool words. "Like" and "ville" are cool words. Here ~~are~~ is a good example. "I'm, like, really hungry. Let's, like, go to lunch-ville."

Rule 5 You shouldn't wear superhero underwear. You may think it ~~be~~ is cool, but it isn't. Trust me on this one.

Rule 6 If you need to read these rules, then you ~~is~~ are probably not cool. You never will be. Cool people don't follow rules. They make the ~~rule's~~ rules!

Highlights of the Speeches at the Hamster Convention, page 28

Martha Washington Hamster

"Fellow hamsters, the time has come for freedom! We ~~would~~ will not live in cages! We will not eat little food pellets! ~~Us~~ We will not drink out of water bottles! Give us liberty, or give us nothing!"

Alexander Hamster

"Hear this, people of the world, hamsters ~~is~~ are tired! We are tired of being ~~pet~~ petted. We are tired of being held. We are tired of being ~~call~~ called cute. We are no longer your pets! We want jobs! We want rights!"

Dollie Hamster

"My fellow hamsters, the enemy is near. We know who they really ~~is~~ are. The~~m~~[y] are cats! They say they just want to sleep and eat ~~my~~ their cat food. But I have seen the look in their eyes. Watch out for all purring sounds!"

Woodrow Wilson Hamster

"We have a good thing here! We get free food! We get plastic houses! We get petted! ~~Is~~ Are you willing to throw all this away? What will you do with this freedom? Will you walk through a house full of cats? Where will you find food? Where will you hide? Be glad you ~~is~~ are a pet!"

Predictions That Never Came True, page 29

The following predictions were made by Magda the Magic, the Great Steve, and Rowena the Wise. None of them came true.

The Great Steve said, "Early next year, a hairbrush will be elected President of the United States."

Magda the Magic ~~say~~ said, "A new law will be ~~past~~ passed that gets rid of all Tuesdays and Thursdays. The new days of the week will be Sunday, Monday, Monday Again, Wednesday, Another Wednesday, Friday, and Saturday."

Rowena the Wise said, "A team of 10-year-old ~~childs~~ children will win the Super Bowl. They will ~~B~~ beat the Green Bay Packers in a close game." (lc)

Magda the Magic said, "Scientists will learn that chickens ~~is~~ are smarter than human beings. A chicken will run for president and lose in a close race~~.~~."

The Great Steve said, "The new fad for children will be cheese dolls. These dolls will have chubby bodies~~,~~ ~~and these dolls will~~ [and will] be made of cheese, and ~~these dolls will~~ make good snacks."

Doorknob Q & A, page 30

Many people today ~~is~~ are confused about doorknobs. This page gives the facts about doorknobs.

Question: Why are doorknobs important?

Answer: Doorknobs are important because ~~it~~ they open doors. If you don't believe this, try opening a door without a doorknob. You'll see how important doorknobs ~~be.~~ are.

Question: My friend Mary is getting a doorknob for ~~his~~ her birthday. Should I g~~o~~[e]t one too?

Answer: Getting your first doorknob is important. Discuss the matter with your parents, a close friend, or a stranger passing by on the street.

Question: Why ~~isn't~~ aren't more doorknobs shaped like bananas or other fruits?

Answer: People might mistake them for real fruits and try to eat the~~y~~[m]. This could be dangerous.

Question: ~~Does~~ Do doorknobs really grow on trees?

Answer: There are doorknob bushes that grow in South America. Most of the doorknobs that grow there are small and ~~didn't~~ don't fit on doors in the United States.

Question: If doorknobs could talk, what would they say?

Answer: One would probably say, "Please turn me. I'm a doorknob~~.~~." Then again, it might say something completely different.

Your Horoscope, page 31

Aquarius: Your sun ~~am~~ [is] lined up with your moon. That means your ballpoint pen will run out of ink. You will also fall in love—with a turtle~~.~~!
Pisces: Do you remember that one thing~~s~~ that you really wanted? Today will be the day that you get it. Then again, it might not. It all depends.
Scorpio: You ~~leaved~~ [left] the back door open. Go close it. Hurry!
Taurus: It ~~be~~ [is] a bad day for a pony ride. If you feel like riding a pony, don't do it. Try riding a bicycle instead, or maybe a ~~largest~~ [large] dog~~.~~.
Sagittarius: Don't even think of leaving any hundred-dollar bills lying around the house. You could lose ~~it~~ [them].
Libra: Your plans for building a 150-story skyscraper may have to be delayed. You should think smaller.
The Rest of the Signs: Today ~~are~~ [is] your lucky day. Don't be surprised if someone ~~walking~~ [walks] up and hands you one million dollars. Stay away from false horoscopes. They are not true.

Dr. Lorna, Pet Psychologist, page 32

Dear Dr. Lorna,
~~Me~~ [I] need your help. My turtle, Willie, ~~are~~ [is] shy. I can't get him to come out of ~~her~~ [his] shell. What should I do?
Signed, Turtle Lover

Dear Shy,
Turtles are stubborn creature[s]. They rarely come out of ~~them~~ [their] shells. Look for events that might interest a turtle, such as basking in the sun or an egg-laying party.
Dr. Lorna

Dear Dr. Lorna,
My teenage cat Sniffles ~~sleeped~~ [sleeps] all day. She won't ~~helped~~ [help] around the house. She won't even watch TV. All she does is sleep and go out to see ~~their~~ [her] friends at night. Should I be worried?
Signed, Worried in Wooster

Dear Worried,
Teenage cats ~~is~~ [are] known for being lazy. Try putting a sprig of catnip under your cat['s] nose. You will be amazed!
Dr. Lorna

New Museums Around Town, page 33

The Museum of Gum
Did you know that there ~~is~~ [are] over 1,500 different kinds of gum? You can see~~n~~ them all in this museum. It includes NBC (Never Been Chewed) gum[,] ~~/~~ [and] ABC (Already Been Chewed) gum displays. Try the cafeteria. There is a complete menu of gum choices for lunch.

The Macaroni Art Museum
This great museum has masterpieces of macaroni art. Some are sprayed with gold[,] ~~/~~ [and] silver paint. There ~~is~~ [are] other kinds of pasta, including spaghetti, little shells, and of course, wagon wheels.

One Billion Dollars
This is not really a museum. It's just a billion dollars in a bigger bag. If you pay extra you can roll around in the money.

The Broken TV and Radio Museum
There are thousands of broken television[s] and radio[s] here. We are proud that none of them work.

Art That Is So Bad You Could Have Made It Yourself
[This is] ~~A~~ museum that ~~have~~ [has] lots of important art. The art is so bad that you could have made it ~~itself~~ [yourself]. You can see finger painting, blobs, smears, and others.

Little Red Riding Hood, page 34

Little Red Riding Hood lived in the forest. One day her mother ~~tell~~ [told] her to take a pot of te~~e~~[a] and three tiny cakes to her granny.
Along came a wolf.
"Who are you[?]" Red asked.
"I'm a wolf," said the wolf.
"A wolf?" said Red. "What's a wolf?"
"Never mind," said the wolf. "If you don't wa[t]ch out, I'll blow your house down[."]
At that point, three pigs came running out of their houses. "Is this guy bothering you?" they ~~ask~~ [asked].
"I'm not sure," said Red. "He told me he was going to blo~~e~~[w] my house down."
[cap] "he ~~could'nt~~ [couldn't] even blow his own nose," said the pigs.
"Oh yeah?" said the wolf. "Watch this."
Well, he blew the house down. But it wasn't Red's house. [cap] it was Granny's house, and ~~Granny~~ [she] was hopping mad.
"Who did this?" Granny cried.
Red and the three pig[s] pointed at the wolf.
"I'm sorry," said the wolf. "I was just trying to prove a point."
"Here, Granny," said Red, handing her the tea and cakes. "They'll make you feel better."
So, the wolf and Granny had tea and cakes.

Diary of a Dog, page 35

Dear Diary,
Today I g~~e~~[o]t up. I did some scrat[c]hing because my neck itched. Then I slept. Then I did some sniffing around. Then I slept. Then I barked at the mai~~l~~man. After that, I took a nap until dinnertime. [cap] for dinner, I had pellets in a dish. [cap] then I went back to sleep.
Yours truly, Louie
Dear Diary,
Today I saw a small white cat~~s~~ out in the yard. This really made me mad! So I barked a lot. I felt better afterwards. Do you know what I ate for dinner[?] I ate pellets! I washed it all down with a big sl~~i~~[u]rp of water. Then I ~~go~~ [went] back to sleep.
Yours truly, Louie
Dear Diary,
I just felt like barking toda~~e~~[y]. So I barked and barked. Then I ~~eaten~~ [ate] pellets and went to sleep.
Yours truly, Louie
Dear Diary,
That mailman comes every day! I'm getting tired of barking at him. But I did it anyway[.] Also, I took a walk. Tomorrow I'll catch up on my sleeping.
Yours truly, Louie

Masterpiece Art, page 36

An Interview with Winnie Van Wonk
Winnie Van Wonk is truly ~~won~~ [one] of the great masters. You look at her work and you are amazed. It ~~wiggels~~ [wiggles] its ears. It seems to be alive! How does she do it?
[cap] I visited Van Wonk's exhibit in Toledo, ohio, on friday. [cap] I asked ~~she,~~ [her,] "How do you do it[?]"
"It's all in the way you hold your hands," she said. She ~~show~~ [showed] me the secret. I couldn't believe it!
Then I asked, "~~What is~~ [What's] next?" She show~~y~~ed me ~~her's~~ [her] new creation.
"I call it the swan," Van Wonk said to ~~I~~ [me].
["]What a genius!" I thought. I still feel that way today!

Answer Key

The Oatmeal Council Presents: New Oatmeal Products, page 37

Here is some great knew oatmeal products. try them soon!

Oatmeal Sneakers
These are high quality athletic shoes maid of oatmeal. You should not exercise on a field that contains milk and butter Your shoes could turn to mush.

Oatmeal Computer
Imagine an entire computers made of oatmeal. The monitor hard drive, and modem are all oatmeal. Because it is made of oatmeal, this computer do not work at all.

Oatmeal Tennis Balls
Play Tennis with balls made of oatmeal. After a few swats, watch the oatmeal fly! It will make you want to play a game at breakfast thyme.

Oatmeal Snow Tires
Mount the tires on your car and go! This great for both trucks and cars! What's the best thing about this? If you get hungy, you can just eat your tires!

This Day in History, page 40

One Year Ago
National Eat Lunch with a Tree Day was declared a holiday on monday, April 2. No one has figured out how you would actually eat lunch with a tree. If they do, this will be a great celebration.

37 Years Ago
The excuse, "The dog ate my homwork" was first used by Timmy Murtz of ogden, ohio. Timmy don't actually have a dog—or any homework, for that matter! His techer didn't believe the excuse for even one second.

50 Years Ago
On august 7, the annoying telephone call were invented in Newark, New Jersey. Homeowners were called and ask if they would like a free offer.

100 Years Ago
Scientest Alexander Graham Baloney said that water is actually not wet. It just seems wet because the other things around it are very dry. His idea were later proved to be purely preposterous.

More Predictions That Never Came True, page 38

The following predictions were made by Magda the Magic, the Great Steve, and Rowena the Wise last year. None of them came true.

Rowena the Wise said, "restaurants will surve pills instead of food. You'ill be able to get a full meal made complete of pills. It will be delicious."

Magda the Magic say, "A band of squirrels will go on a bank-robbing spree and steal millions of dollars. The money will be found in a hollow tree. The squirrels won't never be caught."

The Great steve said, The sun will not rise in the east one morning. It will rise in the north. It will be two hours late. After that, they will learn its lesson and be on time from then on."

Magda the Magic said, "Scientists will discover that fire is actually cold. Campfires will replace air conditioners to keep houses cool"

Rowena the Wise said, "The words 'hello' and 'good-bye' will switch places. 'Hello' will be used to say good-bye to people. And 'good-bye' will be used to say 'hello.' Hello, I must go now."

Things That Tape Might Fix.com, page 41

Welcome to "Things That Tape Might Fix.com."

This is your one-stop source for finding out if tape will fix something. click on any of the choices below to discover things that tape mite fix.

Choice 1: You have capture a wild hippopotamus in the back of your truck. You plan to drive it to a safe place and set it free. But the hippo has brokken through the gate of the truck. Can you use tape to repair the gate?

Answer: Yes, but make sure that you use hippopotamus-strength tape or something stronger.

Choice 2: The dog accidentally teared up your homework. Can you use tape to put it back together again

Answer: You can try, but it still won't change those wrong answers you wrote.

Choice 3: Humpty Dumpty sat on a wall. Humpty Dumpty have a great fall. Can tape put humpty together again?

Answer: All the king's horses and all the king's men couldnt put Humpty together again—even *with* tape.

Choice 4: Slidding into second base, you rip the knee of her jeans. Can you use tape to repair the rip

Answer: Yes, but you're still out!

Playground Sports Report, page 39

Welcome to the Oakland Plaground Sports Report, where we keep you posted on playground sports events.

In hopscotch, Lance Yee hopped and hopped. Then he fall down. "It's not fair!" said Yee. In dodge ball, Cindy Brill got hit on the leg by a ball throne by Tommy Finster. "You're out!" cried Finster. "it didn't hurt a bit," Brill said afterward.

In kickball, Joey Wankel got mad when he didn't get picked for the green team. So he took its ball and went home.

During the morning kickball game, Ginny Pfaff call Timmy Quigley a bad name. Quigley said, "Sticks and stones may brake my bones, but names will never hurt me"

On the jungle gym, Sabrina Sykes did climbed what is now being described as "really, really high." Said Sykes, "That was really, really high!"

On the swigs, Billy Carbury went back and forth a bunch of times. Carbury said, That was really fun."

More Signs of the Times, page 42

this sign was hung on a wall.
Please do not made shadow bunnys, birds, monkeys, people, or any other shadow figures on this wall

This sign were posted on a bathroom mirror.
Plese do not made funny faces in this mirror. This includes Goofy faces, silly faces, and other odd-looking expressions.

This sign was hung in a bedroom.
All teddy bears must be accompanied by a child. We is not responsible for bears who are on her own.